Bhutan

Tom Owen Edmunds

BHUTAN

Land of the Thunder Dragon

VIKING

For Katie, my wife

Mi querida tan talentosa y tan hermosa,
Con cada segundo que pasa cada vez más te amo.

VIKING
Published by the Penguin Group
Viking Penguin Inc., 40 West 23rd Street, New York, New York 10010, USA
Penguin Books Ltd, 27 Wrights Lane, London W8 5TZ, England
Penguin Books Australia Ltd, Ringwood, Victoria, Australia
Penguin Books Canada Ltd, 2801 John Street, Markham, Ontario, Canada L3R 1B4
Penguin Books (NZ) Ltd, 182-190 Wairau Road, Auckland 10, New Zealand
Penguin Books Ltd, Registered Offices: Harmondsworth, Middlesex, England

First American Edition
Published by Viking Penguin Inc. 1988

1 3 5 7 9 10 8 6 4 2

Printed in Spain by
Cayfosa Industria Gráfica, Barcelona

Library of Congress Catalog Card Number: 88-50611

ISBN 0-670-82535-2

Contents

1. Thimphu: Capital of the Dragon Kingdom   41

2. Tsechu: Living Festival   65

3. West: A Glimpse of the Dragon   85

4. North: Abode of the Gods   101

5. Centre: Spiritual Heartland   115

6. South: Jungle-clad Foothills   131

7. East: Forbidden Lands   137

8. Bragpa: Nomadic Yak Herders   151

Land of the Thunder Dragon

For many centuries the outside world had no name for Bhutan. Its lofty frontiers wrapped it in an impenetrable cloak of mystery. When the first British explorers eventually managed to journey there in the eighteenth century they referred to it as Bootan, land of the Booteas – a term thought to have evolved from the Sanskrit 'Bhot ant', meaning 'end of Tibet'. The Tibetan chroniclers of the time referred to Bhutan by many names, including 'Hidden Holy Land', 'the Southern Valleys of Medicinal Herbs' or, most lyrically, 'the Lotus Garden of the Gods'. But if anyone had thought to ask the Bhutanese, they would have been told that their country had always been called *Druk Yul*, literally meaning 'the Land of the Thunder Dragon'.

The Thunder Dragon is a powerful symbol for the Bhutanese: its snarling mouth represents the fearsome strength of the deities that protect Bhutan, and its thunderous roar proclaims the glorious truth of the omnipotent Buddha across the land. Its presence can be seen everywhere: a pair of Thunder Dragons encircle crossed thunderbolts on the national crest, its image appears in every temple and monastery, and most especially in summer its mighty voice perpetually crashes up the valleys, and echoes over darkened mountains, to accompany its gift of life-bringing rain.

It was in the summer that I first visited Bhutan, though being a photographer I think I used a phrase less flattering than 'life-bringing' to describe the torrential rainstorm that greeted my arrival in Paro. Gazing into the teeming foothills, I wondered if in time I would feel like Lord Ronaldshay who, standing on that same spot in 1921, had written, 'We found ourselves, as though caught up on some magic time machine fitted fantastically with reverse, flying back across the centuries into the feudalism of a middle age.'

Bhutan invites such fantastic descriptions. It is, after all, a remote, little known, and largely forbidden, Himalayan kingdom. A land governed from gigantic castle-monasteries called *Dzongs*, whose white-washed walls reverberate with centuries of unseen devotion. A country where archery is the national sport, and where the majority live lives the passage of time has left untouched. Above all, it is a land whose civilisation and culture have flourished beyond the gaze of prying eyes, a land which is enshrined in mystery.

Perched precariously between Tibet to the north, Nepal to the west and India to the south and east, it is to a large extent the physical relief of Bhutan which has dictated its history and allowed it to remain isolated from the rest of the world for so long. To enter, it was necessary to cross either the world's highest and most hostile mountain range, or hack through the malaria-ridden jungle of the plains. Once in Bhutan travel was still by no

A Wheel of Life in Tashichho Dzong, Thimphu, depicting the six realms of reincarnation and the route to heaven and hell.

means easy, as Captain Pemberton realised in 1838 when he wrote: 'The whole of Bootan territory presents a succession of the most lofty and rugged mountains on the surface of the globe,' and added, 'The consequence is that the traveller appears to be shut out on every side from the rest of the world.'

Paro lies in the extreme west of Bhutan. To the north stand the massive peaks of the Great Himalaya separating Bhutan from Tibet, and to the south the precipitous green-cloaked valleys of the Inner Himalaya that peter out eventually on the Indian plains.

This north/south division of Great Himalaya, Inner Himalaya and Southern Foothills essentially holds good for the whole country. Superimposed upon this are three simple lateral divisions of west, central and east Bhutan. The Pele-La Pass through the Black Mountains separates west from central Bhutan, and the fearsome Thumsing-La Pass separates central from east.

The variations in climate stem firstly from these physical divisions, the sub-tropical south giving way to the temperate central zone and ultimately to the frozen peaks of the north, and secondly, to the arrival each summer of the monsoon.

Most Precious Teacher

The early history of Bhutan is rather vague, mainly because most of the written records have been destroyed over the centuries in a tragic series of Dzong fires. However, it is clear that initially Tibet provided the strongest cultural and religious influences, as well as a significant slice of Bhutan's population. In many ways the history of Bhutan is actually the history of the introduction of Buddhism and its different sects – in fact Buddhism is such a powerful, all-pervading force affecting every aspect of Bhutanese life that the two cannot be separated.

Bhutanese history is both complicated and enriched by a vast body of mythology and legend associated with the sacred deeds of its many great saints. But since the seventh century there have been three individuals who have between them largely shaped the character and destiny of the Land of the Thunder Dragon.

The first was Padma Sambhava, usually known by his title *Guru Rinpoche*, which means 'Most Precious Teacher'. It was he who originally introduced Buddhism into Bhutan. Born, the chronicles say, 'of the Lotus Lake' in north-east India, he gained profound knowledge at a young age. He was busily introducing the Nyingmapa or Old Sect of Buddhism into Tibet when King Sindhu of Bumthang invited him to Bhutan, to cure him of a severe illness.

Legend has it that he was brought to Bhutan in 747 A.D. on the back of a flying tiger, which landed near the top of a massive cliff not far from Paro. Here, through meditation, he vanquished the demons that were opposed to the introduction of Buddhism, and then journeyed on to central Bhutan to cure King Sindhu. This he did by staging a festival of ritual dances, many of which are still performed to this day in annual festivals or *Tsechus* all over the country. In gratitude King Sindhu converted himself and his subjects to Buddhism, though the primitive animist spirit worship of the pre-existing Bon religion was not entirely abandoned. Just as the first Spanish priests, when they had problems converting the Indians of South America to Catholicism, simply suggested that they think of the Virgin Mary in terms of their own indigenous deity Pachma Mama or Mother Earth, so in Bhutan many of the ancient beliefs have been incorporated into the faith, and for some religious festivals the presence of a Bon priest or *Shaman* is still considered essential.

The extraordinary impact that the Guru had on Bhutan is everywhere to be seen; in fact, for the Bhutanese, Guru Rinpoche is revered second only to the Buddha himself. Dressed in silk, adorned with precious jewels, and lovingly lacquered in gold, massive statues of the Guru are to be found in almost every temple, and it is his image that graces the most sacred and most ancient religious appliqué tapestries or *Thankas* in the land. Bhutan's most holy temple is dedicated to his memory: it is to Takstang, 'the Tiger's Nest', perched quite breathtakingly on the sheer side of a 3000 foot cliff, at exactly the spot he landed astride his tiger, that every Bhutanese dreams of making a pilgrimage.

For me Takstang, built in 1692, can be counted amongst the wonders of the world. Three times in all I heaved and puffed my way up the precipitous pathways hewn from solid rock by centuries of reverent feet. Each time I was left utterly transfixed by its haunting beauty and by the magnitude of the devotion and skill that must have gone into its construction.

But it was not until my second visit when I attended the annual Paro Tsechu, that I fully realised the extent to which the Bhutanese revere Guru Rinpoche.

Every year whole families will walk for days from their villages in the surrounding hillsides to attend the festival. It consists of five days of spectacular masked dances, folk dances and religious allegorical plays, set in the cobbled courtyards of the ancient Rimpung Dzong, known locally as 'the Heap of Jewels'. So vivid and powerful are the fearsome images that continually flash past you day after day, in great swirls of snarling colour, that by the end I began to picture Heaven and Hell in the same awesome way they had been depicted by the dancers and in the plays.

The climax of this stunning pageant was the appearance, on the afternoon of the fifth day, of a golden figure of the Guru himself. The build-up started well before dawn when, wreathed in darkness, before the entire assembled monk body, an exquisite and very ancient Thanka, measuring 91 by 55 feet, was lowered from the side of a temple. Lit only by the rich flickering light of a hundred or more butter lamps, the massive image of the Guru and his Eight Manifestations gazed down upon the lines of ruby-robed monks, whose heads were bowed and whose bodies swayed gently to the time of the age-old devotional chants.

As the day advanced, and dancing demons were vanquished by heroic deities in terrifying masks, the usually vocal crowd quietened in anticipation of the Guru's arrival. I could feel the tension as his masked retinue danced into the courtyard, and then, suddenly, the great golden figure of Guru Rinpoche appeared. At this the old woman standing next to me gasped and staggered. Clasping her hands together she feverishly whispered, 'Guru, Guru, Guru, Guru...' before, overwhelmed, she threw herself prostrate to the ground. Looking around me, I saw that the rest of the crowd were similarly awe-struck, clearly transfixed by the arrival of the Guru, as if they had just witnessed the second coming.

A first-floor window of a shop in Thimphu's main street decorated with mythical animals

At Whose Feet One Submits

So it was that in the eighth century Guru Rinpoche first united Bhutan in the name of Buddhism, and Bhutan was to wait almost a millennium before the arrival of its second great colossus. The intervening centuries were noted for the emergence of many great saints and an almost perpetual struggle between the different schools of Buddhism for control of Bhutan. Of the saints two are of particular note, both of whom rose to prominence in the late fifteenth century.

The first is the great Pema Lingpa, born in Bumthang as a reincarnation of Guru Rinpoche. He was a well known *Terton*, or 'discoverer of treasures', a title given to those who discovered important teachings of Guru Rinpoche that had been hidden centuries before in times of danger. He is important not only as a much revered saint, born in Bhutan and not India or Tibet, but also because the Bhutanese royal family, whose ancestral home is in Bumthang, are directly descended from him.

The second is the hugely popular Drukpa Kunley, known as the Divine Madman. He has a special place in the affection of the Bhutanese partly for the sacred devotional songs and teachings he passed on, and partly for his extraordinary ability to vanquish evil spirits and demons by displaying his private parts! Still today no house in Bhutan is complete without a brightly coloured phallus hanging from the eaves to protect it from evil spirits.

The sixteenth century saw increasing chaos as internal struggles between the different sects of Buddhism intensified, threatening to tear the country apart. But all this was shortly to change under the mighty Ngawang Namgyal, whose arrival in Bhutan in 1616 was to dominate the history of Bhutan for the next three centuries. Like Guru Rinpoche he came to Bhutan from Tibet, and also like the Guru he is better known by his title, *Shabdrung*, which means 'At Whose Feet One Submits'.

The Shabdrung was the abbot of the great *Drukpa* monastery, Ralung, centre of the Drukpa sect, not far from Lhasa in Tibet. It was during the founding of this monastery that a massive thunder clap, sent it is believed as a sign from Buddha, gave the sect, and subsequently Bhutan, its name, Drukpa, the 'Thunder Dragon Sect'. But the power of the rival *Gelugpa* or Yellow Hat Sect, with the Dalai Lama at its head, was rising so quickly that the Shabdrung, fearing for his life, was eventually forced to flee to Bhutan.

The Drukpa sect, though well established, was only one of several Buddhist schools with a foothold in Bhutan, its chief rival within Bhutan being the *Lhapa* school. However the Shabdrung quickly set about uniting the various Drukpa establishments and with their support managed to increase greatly its influence and power. This was to prove decisive when in 1634 and again in 1639 the king of Tsang in Tibet invaded Bhutan, only to find that the Shabdrung had sufficient support to repel him. It was after his great victory in 1639 that the title of Shabdrung was bestowed upon him, and using his new prestige, he was able to extend the authority of the Drukpa school over most of the country.

The Shabdrung differed from Guru Rinpoche in that he was very much a temporal as well as a spiritual leader. It was he who gave Bhutan its first written laws and set up the network of Dzongs, massively imposing fortress monasteries, from which the country was governed. These Dzongs, found only in Bhutan, are still the focus of both the civil and religious administration of the nation.

When his late majesty King Jigme Dorji Wangchuck decided in the 1960s that a new multi-purpose headquarters was needed to spearhead the development of modern Bhutan, it was a Dzong he built. On the site of an ancient Dzong, originally built by the Shabdrung, he constructed the new Tashichho Dzong. This 'Fortress of the Glorious Religion' dominates the whole Thimphu Valley (page 40) and houses both the National Assembly and the secretariat of the Royal Government of Bhutan, as well as being the summer headquarters of the state monk body. It is through the continued primacy of the Dzong that Bhutan has been able gradually to modernise its economy and yet at the same time lose little of that which is traditionally, and uniquely, Bhutanese.

On my first afternoon in Bhutan, when the storm had cleared, I wandered down the avenue of willows that leads to Tashichho Dzong. As I neared, a stream of busy briefcase-toting civil servants poured down the massive white-washed steps of the Dzong's main entrance. Though they were dressed to a man in immaculate national costume, I could not help but contrast them with the timeless scene I next encountered, as at least fifty tiny barefoot novice monks raced across the cobbled courtyard at the end of the Dzong, their red cloaks luminous in a sudden burst of rich evening sunshine. To me on my first day they seemed two different worlds, but for the Bhutanese the two rest easily side by side.

It was through his network of Dzongs that the Shabdrung was effectively able to unify Bhutan for the first time in its history. The Tibetans again invaded, this time with the aid of Gushi Khan's great Mongol hordes, but in both 1644 and 1647 they were soundly routed by a smaller number of Bhutanese. It is interesting that the emergence of Bhutan as a unified nation came about largely through the need to repel foreign aggression, which must go a long way to explaining why for the next three hundred or more years, Bhutan deliberately decided to isolate itself almost entirely from the outside world.

During this period the theocracy established by the Shabdrung was gradually weakened. He had set up a dual system of government, with civil power vested in a *Druk Desi* (or 'Deb Raja' as the British envoys called him), and religious authority resting with the *Jey Khempo* or head abbot ('Dharma Raja' to the British). The two posts were transcended by the Shabdrung himself as head of state. But when he died in 1651 no clear successor emerged, and to avoid civil disorder his death was kept secret (by claiming he had gone 'into retreat' to meditate) for over fifty years.

Eventually, a triple system of reincarnation was sanctioned, allowing three different individuals all to be reincarnations of the Shabdrung – one representing the Shabdrung's Body, the second his Speech, and the third, who was usually selected as the chief successor, the Shabdrung's Mind. The problem with this system was that since reincarnations are usually recognised in very young children, for the first eighteen years of his reign the new Shabdrung was a minor. The main power thus fell to the Druk Desi, who was often unwilling to relinquish it later. To make matters worse, the district governors, or *Dzongpons* (now known as *Dzongdhas*), often rebelled against the central authority, deciding to rule their own region exactly as they wished.

Thus by the end of the nineteenth century the dual system established by the Shabdrung, which started so admirably, had all but collapsed. It was at this moment, from the seeds of mounting chaos, that Bhutan was to bear its third great son, a leader who was to change the tide of the nation's history.

Precious Ruler of the Dragon People

By the turn of the century two powerful regional govenors, or *Penlops*, dominated the country, the Penlop of Paro in the west and the Penlop of Tongsa, the mighty Ugyen Wangchuck, in the centre of Bhutan. Their rivalry was brought to a head at the time of the famous Younghusband Expedition to Tibet in 1904. The Paro Penlop was in favour of maintaining Bhutan's traditional ties with Tibet, which had now largely fallen under Chinese influence, but Ugyen Wangchuck favoured strengthening Bhutan's links with the British Empire in India. Thus Ugyen Wangchuck, highly regarded by both the British and the Tibetans, became the official intermediary and accompanied Younghusband to Lhasa. There, with his assistance, the historic Anglo-Tibetan Accord which established trade between the two countries was eventually signed.

On his return to Bhutan, it became increasingly clear that Ugyen Wangchuck was the strong, far-sighted leader that Bhutan desperately needed. And so it was that on 17th December 1907, with the unanimous backing of both the civil and religious authorities, the old theocracy was abolished and Ugyen Wangchuck was elected the first hereditary monarch of Bhutan, assuming the title *Druk Gyalpo*, meaning 'Precious Ruler of the Dragon People'.

Today, under the fourth Druk Gyalpo, his majesty King Jigme Singye Wanchuck, the monarchy is not only well established and much loved, but has become a totally integrated part of Bhutanese life and is in many ways the nation's most crucial and dynamic driving force.

The main task of the newly crowned Ugyen Wangchuck (who incidentally was knighted by King Edward VII in gratitude for his part in the Younghusband Expedition) was to consolidate and stabilise the nation's new constitution. On his death in August 1926 this task was taken up by his son, King Jigme Wangchuck. The first two kings undoubtedly achieved a considerable amount, uniting the nation and introducing numerous reforms. However, when the third king, his late majesty King Jigme Dorji Wangchuck, came to the throne in March 1952, Bhutan was still essentially an isolated and feudal land. It was of this ancient society, feudal yet highly developed culturally, that the few early travellers wrote with such fascination.

Good-humoured, downright and thoroughly trusty

In the whole history of Bhutan, right up till 1921, only thirteen foreign missions ever managed to visit the country. The first of these consisted of two Portuguese Jesuit priests, Fathers Cacella and Cabral. They were sent by Father Alberto Laercio, Provincial of the Province of Malabar, East India, to convert Bhutan and Tibet to Christianity. On their way they were robbed twice and imprisoned, but on arrival in Bhutan in 1627 they were fortunate to find there a scholarly and benevolent ruler, the mighty Shabdrung himself. Cacella wrote of the Shabdrung, 'He received us with a demonstration of great benevolence, signifying this in the joy which he showed on seeing us.'

They were to stay with the Shabdrung for several months, living with him in the spectacular hillside monastery of Cheri (page 63) to the north of Thimphu, which the Shabdrung had built in 1619. Cacella describes him as a most devout man, adding, 'This king has also a great reputation as a man of letters and as such all other great Lamas reverence him.'

The priests found the Shabdrung to be remarkably tolerant, allowing them to preach Christianity and even build their own chapel. It appears that the Shabdrung respected

Prayers written on animal skulls in a window of a little chorten in Sakten are thought to help the reincarnation of the dead animal's soul

their religion as another perfectly valid path to spiritual liberation, a most enlightened concept that has sadly taken other religions many centuries to accept, if at all. However, when it came to the crunch the Shabdrung, understandably, said he would rather die than be converted to Christianity himself, and reluctantly he allowed the two priests to continue on their journey to Tibet.

After Cacella and Cabral, there are no records of any other western or eastern travellers reaching Bhutan for well over one hundred years. But by the latter part of the eighteenth century, as the British East India Company's influence expanded further into north-east India, not only contact, but conflict, with Bhutan became inevitable.

With the decline of the Mogul empire the Bhutanese had gained increasing influence in Cooch Behar, a principality to the south. In 1773 Zhidar, the sixteenth Druk Desi, ousted the then ruler Kagenda Narayan and replaced him with a man of his own choice. Narayan fled, and immediately sought help from the British. Warren Hastings, the Governor-General of India, was quick to seize this opportunity to secure the northern frontiers of the Empire. In April 1773 he precipitated the first Anglo-Bhutanese War by signing an agreement with Narayan to reinstate him on his throne, in return for Cooch Behar seceding to the British Empire.

With this Captain John Jones was despatched to Cooch Behar in command of a small force. He succeeded in dislodging the Bhutanese, and also captured two of their forts in the foothills, but in the process he and many of his men died of malaria. There is a splendid engraving of 'Dellamcota Fort in Bootan' in the 1790 Bengal Atlas, with the inscription, 'To the memory of that brave and excellent officer Capt. John Jones; who took it by Afsault (sic) in April 1773, and soon after fell a sacrifice to the unwholesome climate of Coos Beyhar.'

Shortly after this the Panchen Lama of Tibet interceded with Hastings on behalf of the Bhutanese to resolve the dispute. In reply Hastings, hoping to establish new trade routes with the fabled lands of the north, promptly relinquished all Bhutanese territory taken in the campaign, thus paving the way for an unprecedented series of British missions to the area.

The first of these was led in 1774 by the remarkable George Bogle, formerly an officer in the Bengal Civil Service, whom Hastings had appointed his roving ambassador to Bhutan and Tibet. During the five months he stayed in Bhutan he grew very fond of the Bhutanese and came greatly to respect them and their way of life. He wrote of the absence of social stratification in a country where everyone, from the king to the lowliest peasant, wore the same dress, something which still holds good today, and of a people who were 'strangers to falsehood and ingratitude'. He continued, 'Theft, and every other species of dishonesty to which the lust of money gives birth are little known.'

In a farewell message, he wished the Bhutanese lasting happiness that was already denied the peoples of the technically developed nations, who were blinded by the restless pursuit of material gain. And in October 1774, just before his departure, he wrote, 'The more I see of the Bhutanese, the more I am pleased with them. The common people are

Slate carving on a side of a chorten in Thimphu Valley. A red band round a building declares that it is a religious place. The little cones are made of human bones.

good-humoured, downright, and, I think, thoroughly trusty. The statesmen have some of the art which belongs to their profession. They are the best-built race of men I ever saw.'

Just over two hundred years later, having travelled to almost every corner of the country, and having met and lived with Bhutanese from the highest to the humblest in the land, I also left Bhutan with similar feelings. If in 1774 there was a certain magic in Bhutan and the manner of its people that entranced Bogle, then I found it still very much alive today.

An Inexhaustible Fund of Delight

Bogle's mission succeeded in negotiating a trade agreement with Bhutan and Tibet, thus opening the door for further contact. In 1776 and 1777 two missions were led by the surgeon on Bogle's first expedition, Dr Alexander Hamilton, but they appear to have been brief and of no great consequence. However, in 1783 Hastings sent a fourth mission, this time under the leadership of his own relative, Samuel Turner. Accompanying him were Dr Robert Saunders, surgeon and botanist, and Lt Samuel Davis, draughtsman and surveyor, who also painted many fine watercolours.

All three were to leave detailed accounts of their time in Bhutan, which, like Bogle's, I found to be extraordinarily similar to my own observations and experiences. They too were struck by the contrast between the simplicity of daily life, and the complexity and sophistication of the culture and religion – a gulf that is reflected exactly in the contrast between the magnificence of the public buildings and the more mundane (though not insubstantial) rural houses.

Turner exactly described the typical Bhutanese house, a two storey structure made partly of stone and clay, and partly of delicately carved wood forming a balcony, topped with a slatted roof weighed down with boulders. He explained that the ground floor acts as a stable for the hogs, while the space between the dwelling area on the next floor and the roof is used for storing crops. He mentions the rough wooden ladder that leads to the living area on the first floor, and notes how pleasant it is to sit on the balcony, compared with the discomfort of the chimney-less interiors, writing, 'Smoke annoys all present, who at length partake of the same gloomy colour with the ceilings and the walls!'

In contrast Davis writes of the grandeur of Tashichho Dzong, as it was before being rebuilt by his late majesty, and concludes, 'The magnitude, regularity, and showy decorations of this edifice, combined with numerous clusters of houses and well cultivated state of the adjacent land, produced a favourable contrast with the wild and solitary aspect of the country through which the embassy had yet advanced, and afforded a favourable impression of the intelligence and civilisation of the inhabitants of Bootan.'

It was this 'intelligence and civilisation' that also struck Saunders, the scientist on the expedition, leading him to declare, 'I think the knowledge and observations of these people on the diseases of their country, with their medical practice, keep pace with a refinement and state of civilisation, which struck me with wonder.'

Two centuries later I witnessed this alternative medical expertise, in a small way, when visiting an ayurvedic doctor in Bumthang. In jest I held out my hand and asked him if there was anything wrong with me. He held my wrist for a few seconds and then to my astonishment turned to me, frowning deeply, and announced, 'You have had an excess of alcohol.' The previous night I had had my first experience of the locally brewed spirit, which was as Samuel Turner had warned, 'fiery and powerfully inebriating'.

Eventually Turner's mission was given permission to continue its journey to Tibet, and with regret they left Bhutan and its magnificent scenery, of which Turner had written, 'To such as find satisfaction in contemplating nature, in its most gigantic and rudest form, what an inexhaustible fund of delight is here displayed.' What Turner could not have realised, was that he was to be the last westerner for fifty years to witness this grandeur, and that when again it was gazed upon by foreign eyes, it would be by men with harder hearts and harsher words.

The trade routes, so patiently negotiated by these early missions, were suddenly cut by the outbreak of the Sino-Nepalese War in 1792, and not opened again until the Younghusband Expedition in 1904. Vague contact was maintained with the Bhutanese, but it became increasingly tense as both the British and the Bhutanese sought to gain control over the eighteen *duars*, or passes, in Bengal and Assam that were the only means of access to Bhutan from the south.

In 1838 Captain Boileau Pemberton, accompanied by twenty-five men of the Assam Police, crossed into Bhutan, finding it, 'in a state of continual anarchy...and incessant struggles between the Tongsa Penlop and the Paro Penlop.' In words typical of the mounting hostility he described the Bhutanese as, 'indolent to an extreme degree...and victims of unqualified superstition.'

In 1841, not long after Pemberton's expedition, the British annexed the seven duars in Assam, thus starting twenty years of intermittent border clashes that were to lead to the second Anglo-Bhutanese War of 1864-5.

Shortly before the war, the British sent a political mission, under the honourable Sir Ashley Eden, in a last attempt to resolve the dispute. But Eden found the Bhutanese, in the grips of yet more internal disputes, impossible to deal with. In a rather blinkered and marvellously Victorian way, he describes them as 'an idle race, indifferent to everything except fighting and killing one another.'

It appears the Bhutanese could do nothing right and descriptions of his journey make quite unintentionally hilarious reading: 'Some gentlemen of the Mission mounted the animals sent for us, and had a very uncomfortable ride, on high Tartan saddles, on very fidgety and vicious mules. We were preceded by musicians, who continued to play a most monotonous and noisy tune.'

The Bhutanese were clearly not prepared to talk terms with Eden, and the final indignity came when, as described in an article in the *Calcutta Review*, one of the 'ecclesiastical banditti'...'took a large piece of wet barley meal out of his tea cup and, with a roar of laughter, rubbed the paste all about Mr Eden's face. He then pulled his hair, slapped him on the back, and indulged in several disagreeable practical jokes!' The honourable Sir Ashley was clearly not amused. Soon after his return to India, British troops swept up through Bengal and, despite spirited opposition from the Bhutanese, captured all of the eleven remaining duars.

In November 1865 the Treaty of Sinchula ended the war and re-established friendly relations between the two countries. The Bhutanese agreed to waive all claims to the duars, in return for which the British agreed to pay 50,000 rupees a year compensation. The treaty made trade between them open and duty free, thus ushering in a new era for Bhutan during which its attention was gradually to move away from its traditional ties with Tibet, and towards the great Indian subcontinent to the south.

This process was accelerated with the election of Sir Ugyen Wangchuck as the first king of Bhutan; his support for the Younghusband Expedition had clearly demonstrated his desire to extend Bhutan's links to the south. In 1910, shortly after his coronation, he signed a major treaty with the British government in India. In this, the British recognised the sovereign status of Bhutan as an independent country and promised not to interfere in its internal affairs, but in return, Bhutan accepted some guidance in foreign policy matters.

This status quo continued happily throughout the reign of the first two kings, as they consolidated the new constitution internally. But the brutal Chinese invasion of Tibet in 1959 was shortly to shatter Bhutan's tranquillity. It forced the third king to abandon Bhutan's centuries-old policy of self-imposed isolation, in order to seek a place in the larger international community.

Gross National Happiness

Even before the Chinese invasion of Tibet, it was evident within months of his succession in March 1952 that his majesty King Jigme Dorji Wangchuck, the third Druk Gyalpo, had decided it was time for change within Bhutan; time for it to modernise its economy and to ease itself gently into the twentieth century. But acutely aware of the damage that can be caused by a headlong rush to develop, the king wisely decided that these changes must be implemented gradually. His aim was to complement, not destroy, Bhutan's rich cultural heritage.

It is this enlightened outlook to development that dominates the history of modern Bhutan, and continues right up to the present day. The current king perfectly expressed Bhutan's policy when in May 1980 he told *Newsweek* magazine, 'What we want to achieve is a balance between gross national product and gross national happiness.'

The first task facing his late majesty was to set up institutions capable of governing a modern nation. In 1953, a year after his coronation, he established the national assembly, called the *Toshogdu*. This is made up of 150 members, of whom one hundred are freely elected local representatives, ten are nominated by the state monk body, and the last forty are members of the government, appointed by the king. This is the country's main legislative body. It sits twice a year in the capital, Thimphu, in a large and beautifully decorated room standing over one of the main temples in Tashichho Dzong.

In 1956 King Jigme Dorji Wangchuck abolished serfdom and introduced a number of land reforms, and in 1965 he set up a Royal Advisory Council, to which, in 1968, he added the Council of Ministers. In 1968 he also put a motion before the Toshogdu giving it full power to reject ministers, and even the king himself should he fail to pass a vote of confidence. The Toshogdu passed this last section most reluctantly, and in September 1972 it took the first opportunity after the king's death to repeal these votes of confidence in the monarch. Today, his majesty is both head of state and head of the government, but the Toshogdu has the authority to propose any legislation it sees fit.

On the international scene, the last king inherited a treaty of friendship with India signed by his father in 1949, almost identical to that signed by the first king in 1910 with British India. Any doubts as to the interpretation of the clause concerning guidance in foreign policy were to be banished when, in 1971, as a culmination of two decades of gradual change, India sponsored a motion to make Bhutan a full member of the United Nations, which was unanimously accepted by the General Assembly.

Becoming a member of United Nations, as a completely independent and now internationally recognised and ratified sovereign state, was a crucial step for Bhutan. The Chinese invasion of Tibet in 1959 and the Indo-Chinese War of 1962 had opened Bhutan's eyes to the dangers of international isolationism, and to the strategic nature of their country's location. In 1974, the subsequent annexation by India of its other neighbour, Sikkim, must have further enforced Bhutan's desire to seek the fullest possible role in the wider international community. It is today an active member of many international organisations, including the Non-Aligned Movement and the Colombo Plan.

It would be foolish, however, to suggest that Bhutan has anything but the most friendly relations with India. A series of visits by successive Indian Prime Ministers has reaffirmed India's respect for Bhutan's territorial integrity, as well as their desire to assist Bhutan's development. One such visit, by the great Pandit Nehru in 1958, led to the construction with Indian aid of the first metalled road in Bhutan, from Phuntsholing, on the border, to Thimphu. Its completion coincided with the introduction in 1961 of the country's first Five Year Plan, and the measure of Bhutan's economic progress since then is clearly visible as you drive along this road today.

From the road you can glimpse the jewel in Bhutan's economic crown, the massive Chhukha hydro-electric project, that will ultimately generate about 800 megawatts and make Bhutan an energy-exporting nation. A break from the nerve-jangling hairpin bends, at a roadside shop, will reveal some products of new Bhutanese industries: canned fruit juices, bottled jams, and home produced spirits, such as Dragon Rum and the ever-popular Bhutan Mist.

Arrival at the gateway to Thimphu marks also the entrance to the huge modern secondary school where, if you were to enquire, you would be told that Bhutan boasts a total of over 125 schools, as well as a number of technical colleges, and that plans are afoot for the development of a fully-fledged university. Continuing over the bridge, towards the beautiful *chorten* (religious monument) built to honour the memory of his late majesty (page 55), you may just spot Thimphu's modern hospital, one of thirteen in Bhutan, not including over forty dispensaries and many more basic health units located all over the country.

Shortly before reaching your hotel you may catch a glimpse of the ornate bank of Bhutan building on the right, before a near miss with a suicidal betel-chewing lorry driver will complete your education, reminding you in an instant that Bhutan has a fleet of trucks to carry essential goods over a thousand miles of new highways.

Bhutan has indeed achieved much since that first Five Year Plan but there is, of course, a long way to go: despite progress in health care there is still a high rate of infant mortality, and diseases such as malaria, goitre, tuberculosis and leprosy are not uncommon, and in spite of the rapid expansion of schools the literacy rate has yet to rise much above 10%. However, while serious crime in Bhutan is still almost unknown, it does share one major western malaise, a surprisingly high divorce rate – though this can be attributed more to the relaxed attitude of the Bhutanese towards marriage and the lack of any stigma surrounding divorce, than to outside influence.

But development itself has brought new problems, and raised new questions. At what speed should reforms be implemented? What of the old should be replaced, and what of the new rejected? In reality making such selections cannot be so cut and dry – how can one have a central bank generously set up with Indian aid and expertise, without inheriting the bureaucracy? But once the development process is under way it cannot be stopped: one step leads irresistibly and inevitably to the next, and there is the ever-present danger that the natural momentum of change itself will take control.

But to date the Bhutanese have been remarkably successful. They have taken great strides forward, without seeming to have damaged the fabric or the spirit of their own culture. The best example of this can be found in Bumthang, where the modern hospital happily co-exists right alongside the traditional practice. Patients can choose between the two, and, if not satisfied, they can try next door!

However, partly because of the government's specific concern to bring about change within the confines of the traditional Bhutanese way of life, and partly because of the extreme inaccessibility of much of the country, despite all that has changed, one does not have to venture far to find oneself immersed in a way of life that has remained unaltered for centuries.

Detail of wall painting of the Buddha of a thousand arms and a thousand eyes in Punakha Dzong.

The Nature of the Dragon

It is the ancient, traditional Bhutan, of which the Bhutanese are so proud, and which they have taken such trouble not to destroy, which forms the subject of my photographs. I do not deny the advent of change, nor the benefits it has brought, but feel there is time enough to record these changes later. This is not to say that I have ignored the real Bhutan, and snatched isolated pictures from a vanishing past. Rather it is exactly the opposite. In a country where 95% of the population still live by traditional agriculture in remote scattered hamlets, unaltered by the passing centuries, it is *their* Bhutan, which they are still living day by day, that is the *real* Bhutan.

That the Bhutanese government recognise this, is demonstrated by their compulsory system of 'national service'. The brightest Bhutanese students, who have been abroad to receive further education, are sent, on their return, to live in a village for several months, to remind them of the lives, and the needs, of the ordinary people: the people whom they will shortly be serving in their new jobs in the government administration.

My two journeys in Bhutan were to take me through many such villages, some of which had never before seen foreigners. These were on my first trip from Thimphu in the west, across the entire breadth of the country, to the isolated villages of Mera and Sakteng on the eastern border. The east of Bhutan is effectively off limits for tourists purely because the infrastructure to cope with them does not exist. I was only allowed to travel there because I was most fortunate to have been invited to Bhutan as a guest of a member of the royal family, whom I had met in India. The centre of Bhutan is almost as untouched as the east, though in the last few years it has gradually been opened up.

It was in 1974 that the government decided to admit tourists for the first time. Wanting the revenue, and eager to promote international awareness of Bhutan, they were nevertheless wary of the impact that a large number of tourists can have on a small unspoilt population, and thus decided to allow in only a small annual quota of tourists, to be charged a relatively large sum per head. They are formed into groups and escorted by a well trained guide, who takes them to the most interesting places in the west of the country. Currently two thousand tourists are admitted a year, though this will increase as facilities expand, and new itineraries, including specialist trekking and adventure tours, are always being introduced.

My numerous visits to Thimphu demonstrated how successful Bhutan's tourist policy has been so far. Twelve years after the first tourists set foot there, I was still not once asked to change dollars, to hand out sweets, to buy any trinkets from street hawkers, or least of all, hastled for 'baksheesh'.

But one can only be fearful for the future. As the number of tourists grows so will their impact. The problem is not so much the isolated incidents of genuinely bad behaviour, such as the aggressive shoving aside of monks at the Tsechu to get photographs, but much more the biros and sweets handed out with the very best of motives. A relationship that starts as genuine interest and mutual curiosity soon becomes, 'Will I get a biro from this one?', and conversely, 'Will I be pestered for sweets by this little boy?'. Local people start to be perceived as nuisances who bother you to give them things, and visitors in their turn as people who are aloof, often mean and invariably patronising. From this only further deterioration follows.

That this has *not* yet happened in Bhutan is due partly to the excellent tourist policy (limited numbers and strict rules such as 'no tipping'), partly to the restraint shown by and large by tourists (who realise they have a responsibility in visiting somewhere so uniquely unspoilt), and partly to the robust character of the Bhutanese. There is no headlong rush to abandon their beliefs and way of life for ours, because for them, there is no sense of racial or cultural inferiority – in fact, exactly the opposite. It is pleasant enough to have us visit and tell them how wonderful their country is, and how we wish we hadn't spoilt our own, but we are a pretty ignorant bunch really. What do we know of the ancient mysteries of the all-powerful Buddha?

But sadly I can think of no country where the relationship between tourist and resident has not eventually been soured to some extent. Having said that, I also cannot think of a country that has such a far-sighted tourist policy, and one can only hope that the honeymoon will last.

For my part, I found the people in Thimphu just as open and friendly as those I met in the remotest villages of eastern Bhutan, who honoured our progress by lighting fragrant juniper fires at shrines along our way.

My first trip covered less than 150 miles as the crow flies, but the rugged nature of the terrain meant the journey took over a month. We started at 7,500 feet in the fertile Thimphu Valley, crossed passes at over 13,000 feet cloaked in perpetual monsoon mist, to arrive in Tashigang, Bhutan's most easterly town, at a sweltering 3000 feet. Not one day would pass during which we would not be permanently climbing up one hill, in order to climb down the other side, only to be confronted by the next!

In the spring or autumn it is sometimes possible to make this journey in just two days, by four-wheel drive vehicle, along the partially tarmacked lateral road. But in the summer, continual landslides brought on by torrential rain effectively block the road. So from Bumthang, in the heart of Bhutan, where the 'black-top' ends, we travelled the rest of the way on foot and by mule, along ancient tracks through the forests and across fields of ripening buckwheat.

It was here that I felt I had reached the essence of Bhutan. We passed lines of young girls carrying woven baskets of newly cut barley, and barefoot elderly men labouring under herculean loads of firewood; we saw brightly coloured talismans standing guard in the fields, protecting the crops from evil spirits, and passed at almost every step a prayer flag gaily fluttering in the wind, a red-banded chorten built to honour the memory of some long past but much revered saint, or a prayer wall round which an old lady paced with penitent steps. We were never far from the sound of rushing water, the constant chatter and cry of a thousand unfamiliar birds, the sound of a dog barking in a distant hamlet carried miles on the strong wet wind, and occasionally the haunting melodic resonance of a trumpet accompanied by the stately boom of an ancient drum, punctuating the progress of a *puja* or religious ceremony. We may stop for a day as a guest of a mighty Dzongdha, in one of the massive gilded Dzongs from which he administered his region, then pass on to stay the next with a village headman, stretching out on irregular wooden floor boards, in a smoke-blackened room that housed the family shrine, with the low, gentle grunting of the pigs in the stable and the constant pounding of the rain on wooden windows gradually lulling us to an exhausted sleep.

As we progressed, we passed from land in the west dominated by the Drukpa people, of mongoloid origin, who speak the national language Dzongkha, the language of the Dzongs, to the central valleys, where Bumthangpha is commonly the first language, and finally into the land of the Sharchops, where Sharchopkha is the mother tongue. However, in eastern Bhutan alone, there are said to exist eleven different dialects, many of which are mutually unintelligible. This is one of the reasons that we had to have a guide, but even he, who spoke twelve different Bhutanese languages, was sometimes caught out by dialects that could be restricted to a small cluster of hamlets at the top of a single valley.

The climax of our journey was when we became two of just a handful of foreigners ever to have been permitted to travel further east, beyond Tashigang, to visit the remote yak-herding Bragpa peoples in the isolated villages of Mera and Sakteng (pages 150–160). It is these people, of Tibetan origin, who wear the yak felt hats with five points to guide the rain of this stormy region away from their faces, and the magnificent animal skins slung over their home-spun clothes. They are the most noble and fine-featured race, living half the year high up in the mountains grazing their yaks on the alpine pastures, returning in winter to the sheltered valleys to ride out the snows.

We visited them at the height of summer when they were living in their two main villages: tightly clustered settlements of fifty or so small stone houses, nestling in the middle of steep slopes of fine cropped grass. The children spent the day sitting in these pastures in ones and twos playing games with pebbles and tending to the herds of shaggy black yaks. The men would chop wood, carve up a freshly slaughtered carcass, or be out shepherding their herds on the higher and more remote pastures, while the women dried grain in the sun, milked the yaks to make the butter and cheese for which they are renowned all over Bhutan, or wove their fine home-made cloth on the simple hand looms outside their houses.

The village seemed to be constantly moving, an impression given partly by the natural daily bustle of village life and partly by the Bragpa habit, shared by both men and women, of spinning wherever they went; dropping their twirling wooden spindles, jerking them up again, pulling a fresh length of rough wool from the stock twisted around their arm and then repeating the process. Looking down on a packed village meeting, the sense of perpetual motion was almost overpowering, as a sea of arms rose, fell and twisted, heads bobbed sideways exchanging snippets of local gossip, and little children in their own tiny animal skins raced about between their cross-legged, ever-twirling mothers.

We stayed with the Bragpas for several days. We were welcomed into their homes, shown amazing hospitality and courtesy, and treated with a fascination equal to that which we found in them.

Throughout this first trip I was accompanied by an English writer, Katie Hickman, whose long blonde hair and strange clothes stuffed with feathers were the subject of special curiosity amongst the Bragpas. On her return to England, Katie wrote a book called *Dreams of the Peaceful Dragon*, published by Victor Gollancz, about our experiences on this extraordinary journey. As there is no substitute for reading her original account, I will dwell no further on this first expedition. But less than a year later, I was very fortunate to find myself once again at Calcutta Airport boarding an eighteen seater plane, bound a second time for the Land of the Thunder Dragon.

Cosmic mandala, depicting the Bhutanese view of the universe, on a wall in Rimpung Dzong in Paro.

The Dragon Revisited

This time my arrival at Paro in early March was greeted by brilliant sunshine, and that crystal freshness in the air found only in the mountains. It was in stark contrast to the oppressive heat I had encountered where my journey had actually started, in the magnificent jungles of Manas Wildlife Sanctuary on the Indian/Bhutanese border, many miles to the south-east.

It was standing on the white-pebbled banks of the Manas River during a trip to India seven years earlier, gazing across at the foothills rising sheer from the opposite bank, cloaked in dark impenetrable jungle and a lingering wispy mist, that I first set eyes on the legendary kingdom of Bhutan. It was to fulfil a promise I had made to myself at that moment, that I now returned to Manas at the beginning of my second expedition to Bhutan.

Manas Wildlife Sanctuary, lying half in India and half in Bhutan, is one of more than a dozen national parks established as part of the Project Tiger Campaign in the early 1970s. It is split in two by the Manas River, the Indian half being mainly flat and covered in dense forest with patches of elephant grass, the Bhutanese side being mountainous and jungly. It is a haven for the tiger, but so dense and impenetrable that it is seldom seen. Instead Manas is better known for its scenic beauty, and as the only home of the extremely rare and very beautiful golden langur (page 134), a monkey whose global range is restricted to one tiny pocket of forest on the Bhutanese side of the reserve.

I stayed in the Bhutan Forest Lodge, part of a small complex of foresters' buildings in a clearing, perched over a bend in the river. On arrival, sitting on the verandah at dusk as the lone occupant of the lodge, I could quietly look out over the river to the mountainous jungles beyond, watching the colours slowly mellow and ripen as the sun fell. The loud feathery 'whoosh whoosh' of the giant pied hornbill's return to roost gradually gave way to the more silent and sinister silhouette of the Indian flying fox, a fruit-eating bat with a body the size of a squirrel and a wingspan to match. The appearance of these 'birds of the night' in the fading inky sky heralded the start of the noisy nocturnal chorus, the deep lazy grunt of the bull frogs and the urgent harsh metallic piping of the cicadas setting the relentless rhythm of the jungle night.

The best way to see Manas is on elephant back. It is both easier and safer than walking, and infinitely more enjoyable. Every morning about an hour before dawn I would climb the wooden mounting post and unsteadily lower myself into the howdah, before swinging off rather drunkenly towards the forest. For me, elephants lumber. Perched on top, one rolls very gently from side to side in a most stately and dignified motion, ducking out of the way of dewy overhanging branches, and peering down intently into the gloom from an unaccustomed height of fifteen feet.

I was constantly amazed by how quiet our progress was through the jungle, the loudest noise being the 'wooosh-slap' of the elephant's ears flapping against its body (a noise that can be exactly reproduced by holding a wellington boot by the bottom and slapping the top against your knee!), accompanied by the leathery creaking of ancient harnesses, the rustle of vegetation and the occasional command barked by the mahout. I spent many a happy morning amongst the wakening animals, which were virtually undisturbed by my presence aboard such a familiar form, slowly rolling from side to side and wooosh-slap, wooosh-slapping my way through the forest.

Midday was the quietest time in the Manas. A heavy heat settled on the jungle, no breeze shook the branches, few animals stirred in the undergrowth, the only sounds were a mournful hollow 'hoop hoop' of a distant bird, the occasional sharp scurrying of a lizard in the leaf litter, and – the only sound that never changed – the eternal restless pounding of the river.

As I crossed the Manas River for the last time the harsh, cat-like 'peeyow' of the peacocks announced the end of both the daily forest siesta and the first leg of my trip. After two days of jeep, train, taxi then plane I found myself circling over Paro Dzong marvelling at the rich blue sky and snow-dusted peaks that had been permanently shrouded on my first trip.

On arrival it transpired that my visa was not entirely in order. While the customs officer sorted it out, rather than being put in a detention room I was brought tea on a tray and treated with extraordinary courtesy. This small incident is typical of the hospitality one receives in Bhutan and it was to set the tone for the whole of the rest of my trip.

The scene as I drove to Thimphu was a strange mix of the familiar and the unfamiliar. The familiar was the sight of the sizeable mud brick and wooden houses, with their boulder-laden slatted roofs and small painted windows, set in a patchwork terrace of irregular fields, newly sown with rice and barley; and the distinctive stature and dress of the Bhutanese. Both men and women have short, closely cropped dark hair above open mongoloid faces; the women wear *keras*, ankle-length dresses of a single piece of material, held with silver clasps on each shoulder, and the men home-spun *khos*, like tartan dressing gowns with big pouches in the front (holding a small wooden bowl, a day's supply of betel nut and other essentials), and a rough wooden-sheathed knife thrust jauntily into the waist band. The unfamiliar lay in the parched brown hillsides (so different from the intense green of summer), the blue skies and the clear crisp air. It was wonderful to be back.

Thimphu had certainly changed little in my absence. There is one main street of shops, beautifully painted traditional Bhutanese houses (page 48) into which one leans, through the window, pointing into the gloom at the higgledy-piggledy goods inside. After Tashichho Dzong and the Memorial Chorten, both of which I visited many times, my favourite location in Thimphu was the Sunday market. Every week a huge mass of people would walk for hours, sometimes days, heaving great loads of vegetables and all sorts of other merchandise to sell at the colourful confusion of the market (pages 49–53).

What struck me most was the range of peoples that it attracted; it was cosmopolitan, but in a very Himalayan way, rather as Timbuctoo in its heyday would have been very cosmopolitan in a Saharan way. There were Tibetans with plaited grey hair tied up over their heads, and large rough turquoise earrings; Nepalis with brightly sparkling gold nose-studs, or colourful jaunty skull caps; Indians with long billowing saris in dazzling primary colours, made of the finest silk; Sikhs with their distinctive turbans, and beards beautifully oiled and groomed; no doubt the odd Sikkimese, and, of course, a multitude of Bhutanese in every guise, monks in their bright ruby cloaks testing tempting selections of shiny new cymbals and ornate silver trumpets, and well-to-do wives in their Sunday best keras bargaining with barefooted farmers over baskets of cheeses.

I had timed this second trip to coincide with the great Paro Tsechu and the fine spring weather. In Bhutan the winter is cold and often snow-bound, the summer being warmer, but wet and very prone to landslides. The best seasons to travel are spring and autumn when the roads and the skies should be clear. Unfortunately this is not as simple as it sounds as, being a mountain country, Bhutan is notoriously prone to what is commonly termed 'unseasonal weather'.

There is nothing, however, unpredictable about the Paro Tsechu – it has started at the same time, on the eleventh day of the second month of the Bhutanese lunar calendar, and followed almost exactly the same pattern, for centuries. Some of the masks worn are said to be two hundred years old, but the dances themselves are much older. One of the most spectacular, the Dance of the Lords of the Cremation Grounds (page 70), was exactly described by Samuel Davis in 1783, though it has probably remained unchanged since the Shabdrung himself first composed it. Other dances, such as the Dance of the Ging and Tsholing, can be traced as far back as the eighth century, to their introduction by the sacred Guru Rinpoche.

The Tsechu, held annually in all Dzongs, is the highlight of the religious calendar, but it is also the great carnival of the year, a chance for all the local people to meet up, exchange news, show off their finest clothes, and take a break from the rigours of daily life. It is usually held either in the spring, at the end of a bitter winter, or in autumn, when the harvest has been safely gathered in – so they are also a time for celebration. Tsechus, all over Bhutan, are very much more than mere tradition: they are living festivals, the Paro Tsechu being the greatest of them all.

It was not until I returned to England much later, and was watching a production of *Romeo and Juliet* in the Open Air Theatre in Regent's Park, that I was unexpectedly reminded of the Tsechu. As the drama unfolded I suddenly realised that, excepting dress and race, the crowd at the Tsechu was exactly the same as that which would have seen the very first Shakespeare productions. The daily preoccupations and seasonal rhythm of the lives of Shakespeare's original audiences and the spectators at the Tsechu, would have been identical. Having so recently sat amongst such a crowd in Paro, the play took on an entirely new dimension – as I had met the audience for which it had been written.

Beyond the Blooming Vale

When the festival was over, its images gradually faded as I prepared for the main phase of the trip, a trek to the frozen far north of Bhutan.

As the crow flies, the distance from my starting in Punakha to the remote village of Laya on the Tibetan border is less than thirty-five miles. But to walk there and back was to take nearly two weeks. The explanation is quite simple – the Himalayas. In just ninety miles Bhutan stretches from peaks of 24,000 feet in the north to a mere 600 feet in the south. I had started at 600 feet in Manas, and it was now time to walk north.

Punakha lies at 5000 feet, significantly lower than Thimphu to the west, and is well known for its benign climate. Referred to in the ancient chronicles as 'the Blooming Vale of the Luxuriant Fruits of the South', it houses one of the finest Dzongs in Bhutan, built by the Shabdrung in 1637. Standing on an island at the confluence of the Pho Chu and Mo Chu, the male and female rivers, it serves as the winter headquarters of the Jey Khempo and the state monk body.

Wall painting in Tashigang Dzong, with a more Oriental/Chinese style, East Bhutan

On the last day of March, when I arrived, Punakha should have been basking in the warm sunshine of early spring. Instead it was cloaked in a dismal, discoloured haze that had hung mournfully over the whole valley for days. It is possible that it was merely another burst of 'unseasonal weather', but I have a feeling that the valley was indeed in mourning. In February a fire had broken out in the Dzong which had totally gutted the Jey Khempo's quarters. For the Bhutanese this was an extremely bad omen.

The haze accompanied us throughout our first day, but by dawn of the second we were in the mountains and on our way. My hostess had sent with me a guide called Ugyen who, apart from being excellent company, had also, most fortuitously, been assistant chef at the Bhutan Hotel in Thimphu. He was in charge of hiring the horses and horsemen, whom he then loaded down with huge boxes of supplies.

Ugyen turned out to be something of a miracle worker – not only did he manage without fail to get us to our destination each evening, but on arrival he would conjure up, come rain or snow, a mammoth feast right from the midst of his muddy sacks and ancient wooden boxes. There was something splendidly incongruous about sitting cross-legged in front of a campfire, in the faltering twilight of a remote Bhutanese valley, eating fresh asparagus soup, followed by sweet and sour chicken with red rice, then yak meat and onion stew, potatoes dauphinoise, and spinach in cheese sauce, rounded off by fruit salad with cream and brandy! Despite my vigorous nightly protests he never once let standards slip, much, I expect he realised, to my delight.

If my meals were not exactly à la Livingstone, the terrain, at least, came a little closer. We started in the Pho Chu valley, whose dark forested slopes were so impossibly steep that the sun scarcely struck the white angry torrent below for more than a few minutes a day, before returning it once more to its primeval twilight. Beyond the ridges of the valley stood more ridges, and beyond them more again, each seeming steeper and more threatening than the next, like the exaggerated relief of an eighteenth century engraving. For almost two days we trudged up this valley, unable to lower our gaze from these colossi of creation.

When we did eventually emerge it was to the welcoming reassurance of a broad fertile valley sculptured by terraced paddies and spotted with friendly, familiar hamlets. Once again I was immersed in the age-old traditional life of the Bhutanese peasant farmer.

While the fields dictate the rhythm of the village year, it is the family unit that provides the focus of village life. Within the family there is a great equality between the sexes, and the generations: both men and women work in the fields and both look after the children, it being common to see men and women carrying babies on their backs; the grandparents will live alongside their grandchildren in the family house, the different generations playing an equal role in the respect and the running of the household.

Cultivation is done on a communal basis. Each farmer owns his particular fields, but when the time comes to plough, or sow, or harvest, the village will group together, working in rotation on all the different households' fields. No payment is made for working on somebody else's fields, as within the next few days he or she will be working on yours. The only responsibility of the owner is to feed everybody for that day. The typical village will be almost self-sufficient, growing all the food it needs, weaving its own cloth, and constructing its houses from local materials. Any items it cannot get, such as chillies or wool, it will trade for, say, rice.

This absence of a monetary economy, at least until recently, has led to a strange statistical anomaly whereby for years Bhutan had almost the lowest Gross National Product per capita of any country in the world, yet the people themselves were considerably better off than those of a great number of other nations. Financially Bhutan is a poor country, but its people are certainly not starving. In fact, any Bhutanese who does not have a house and four acres of land has the right to seek an audience with the king and ask for his assistance, and once, on my first trip, we gave a lift to somebody who was travelling to Thimphu to do exactly that.

However, this is not to suggest that Bhutanese life is all singing communally in the paddies. It is a very hard, very tough, and often very short, life. Yet the Bhutanese are highly resilient and extremely good-humoured, and travelling through the countryside one cannot help getting the impression of a certain peace and harmony – indeed, one of my most powerful memories of Bhutan is of a sound that carried up the hillsides on those breezy early April afternoons, the sound of people singing in the fields.

After an easy day's walk we reached the famous Gasa Hot Spring, a place of pilgrimage for many Bhutanese. They come from all over Bhutan to rest and bathe, or to seek a cure for an ailment. From the hot spring it was just two hours, but an almost vertical climb, to the magnificent Gasa Dzong (page 103), the halfway point on our journey to Laya.

Gasa's other main claim to fame is that the Shabdrung's chief disciple, who brought him safely from Tibet, was a local boy. But it was not just in gratitude for this that the Shabdrung built the Dzong in 1649, for Gasa is a superb natural fortress, a perfect place from which to repel Tibetan invasions. Built on a craggy outcrop halfway up a mountain, it is surrounded on every side, as far as the eye can see, by the awesome jagged peaks of the Great Himalaya.

To continue on our journey northwards we had to cross the lofty Laga Panchu Pass, the last remaining obstacle. Though it was to be our most arduous day, it was also by far the most beautiful: the pathway to the pass lit by startling bursts of red, mauve, pink and white, the hallmark of a rhododendron forest in flower. Exotic crested pheasants, deep metallic blue with red eyes and fan-shaped tails, strutted nervously in the undergrowth, and the air was filled with great bubbling crescendos of strange bird song. We even caught a glimpse of a bear, a tiny black furry bundle, lolloping on all fours ahead of us on the path. The horsemen, who live in mortal fear of bears, yelled at the top of their voices, and it stopped, turned its elongated beary snout in our direction, and scampered for cover as fast as its little legs could carry it.

As we climbed, we passed caravans of panting shaggy yaks, hooves crashing and bells jangling, heaving loads of butter and cheese from the high mountain pastures. The lead yak, who knew the path, was adorned with a bright red shock of hair on its forehead, and was followed by its masters, who yelled, cajoled, and whooped loud echoed greetings at their fellows along the path.

Slowly the air began to thin, and the temperature dropped noticeably. The jagged snowy peaks on the other side of the valley gradually drew closer and closer, till it seemed that we could almost reach out and touch them. They were solitary, foreboding summits: their valleys uninhabited; their peaks unnamed and unclimbed, the exclusive abode of fearsome local deities.

As we neared the pass a strange silence seemed to grip the forest; there was no breeze to stir the leaves, the birds ceased to call, and even the distant thunder of the river gradually faded to nothing. It seemed as if we had trespassed into some monstrous prehistoric world, a world beyond the realms of sound.

As we turned a corner the spell was broken, a fierce gust of misty wind whistled over the

Statue of Guru Rinpoche aboard his flying tiger, in a temple at Takstang Monastery, where he is believed to have landed in A.D. 747, bringing Buddhism to Bhutan

last remnants of the winter's snow, sending a solitary prayer flag into a noisy frenzy. We had crossed the Laga Panchu Pass.

We camped in a small valley three hours below the pass, arriving just in time to pitch our tents. After my usual light supper, I clambered into both my sleeping bags, quietly confident that little could stop us reaching Laya the next evening. I had not, however, anticipated waking up at 3 a.m. with the top of my tent lightly resting on my nose.

There were only two explanations: either I had slept standing up, or my tent had collapsed. After a gargantuan struggle I freed one of my hands from the midst of my sleeping bags and gingerly prodded my tent. To my amazement, it was weighed down by what I approximated to be about twelve feet of snow. Two inches more, I mused in my rather melodramatic half-wakefulness, and the world would have been one slightly rotund photographer less. Frantically I erected my tripod, and having placed it over my head to avoid being smothered by any further collapse, I fell once more into a blissful sleep. It was in this repose that Ugyen, having fought his way through the snow drifts with a cup of tea, found me the next morning. It was, I gathered from a rather startled Ugyen, all most unseasonal.

Despite this early set-back we did in fact reach Laya later that day. After two hours walking upwards and eastwards, we swung round to the north for the last time, entering a succession of interlocking valleys as steep as before, but on a much smaller scale. Amongst the enormity of the surrounding mountains these valleys, getting smaller and steeper as they progressed, seemed to be guiding us inexorably towards some secret inner sanctum. Just beyond the last stood the village of Laya.

Like the Bragpas of Mera and Sakteng, the people of Laya are also yak-herders of Tibetan origin, and are also sometimes referred to as Bragpas. But their language, a dialect of old Tibetan, their dress and their surroundings are markedly different (pages 100–113). Instead of yak felt hats the women wear sharply conical straw hats with a cross at the top, dark shawls and long patchwork skirts. The men wear the kho, but with a woolly Chinese hat with fold-down ear muffs, to keep out the bitter cold.

Standing at about 11,500 feet, Laya is one of the highest villages in Bhutan. Perched on the side of a steep slope facing, just over the valley, three huge snow capped hills, it is also one of the most spectacular. It lies scarcely more than five miles from the border and, on a clear day, the massive mountains of Tibet seem just a short brisk walk away.

As we passed through the stone archway, with its roughly hewn wooden male and female figures which protect the village, the snow once again began to fall. In a field to the left two old ladies continued hoeing the soil, oblivious to both us and the snow, stooped figures wrapped in long black shawls. Two younger girls in the next field were considerably less oblivious, shouting in raucous high-pitched voices to their friends, before dissolving into peals of helpless giggles.

Soon a gaggle of children had gathered nervously around us, not daring to come too close, while their elder sisters shrieked and shouted and giggled some more. Unlike other Bhutanese, the women of Laya have very long, very dark hair, worn loose over their coarse dark shawls and rough silver necklaces. This, combined with their naturally fine features, gives them an extraordinary wild beauty.

Even though 'beauty' may not have been the term that they were applying to me with such merriment, whatever it was, it was most certainly good-natured. Our horsemen exchanged greetings with the girls, prompting yet more shrieks and giggles, while the men smiled and nodded, and continued ploughing in the gathering gloom. As we slowly trudged up the pathway between the fields, the village headman came out to meet us. Through the quickening snow he led us to the monastery where we were to stay, and in formal tones welcomed us to the village of Laya.

In April there were two main activities in Laya, both concerned with preparing the fields to be sown with barley: the men ploughing the terraces with rough wooden ploughs drawn by pairs of yaks; the women, in groups of three to five, carrying loads of manure from the stables in woven straw baskets slung on their backs. Come sun or snow, or in some cases blizzard, the work continued, with yells of encouragement to straining yaks, and echoed greetings between lines of girls, wafting up the valley. The elder women would milk the yaks and look after the smallest children, and in the evening greet those returning from the fields with great pots of steaming hot water to wash in, ladled out with a huge wooden spoon, before shepherding them upstairs to sit by the fire. I tagged on to the line of girls with their baskets, walked with the men as they struggled with their yaks, and washed my hands in the steaming evening cauldron – always welcomed, wherever I wandered, with a cheerful, curious smile.

Well before dawn, on the day we were to leave, I slipped and stumbled through the pale, icy blue light, to await the sunrise on a small hill overlooking the village. Hanging silent over ghostly blue mountains, I watched the rare, cloudless stillness of a star-filled night gradually fade into the first weak wakenings of a new day.

As a distant mountain caught the first blood red ray of dawn, the village began to stir. A yak shook itself of overnight snow and rose on stiff, unsteady legs. A dog barked, welcoming its household to the coming day, and gradually, as the sun yellowed and strengthened, the village came to life.

With the familiar sounds of a Laya day floating up to my eyrie, I reflected on the Bhutan of which I had become so fond. A vision of the mythical Shangri-la came irresistibly to my mind. But the Bhutanese, I knew, do not welcome this image, finding it patronising and simplistic. Bhutan, they declare, is a real country, with real people, and of course they are right.

Yes, I thought, as I skidded my way back down to the village, they are right. Bhutan is definitely not Shangri-la.

'Not Shangri-la,' I shouted to a rather startled passing yak, waiting until it was well out of ear-shot, before adding quietly to myself, 'But very, very close.'

The Bhutanese national crest, with the Thunder Dragon encircling crossed thunderbolts, in Tashichho Dzong, Thimphu

Acknowledgements

In many ways just one acknowledgement would be sufficient, as without the incredible hospitality and unceasing assistance of Her Royal Highness Ashi Cheoki Wangchuck and her husband H. E. Dasho Topga Rinpoche Yulgyal this book would not have been possible. Never before have I experience such extraordinary kindness – my debt and affection for them goes beyond words. Thank you, Ashi and Topga, so much.

My thanks also go to their daughters Ashi Sonam and my dear friend Ashi Deki Chhoden, as well as to Ashi Pem Dechen, Ashi Deki and Dasho Sangay, Ashi Pema and Dasho Pasang, Uncle Nado, Ugyen Rinzin and Benchen Khempo for all their help and friendship, and also to Pema Tshomo and Rinzin.

Very special thanks also to my two wonderful guides and companions: Karma Tenzing whose courageous persistence got us to the far east of Bhutan, and Ugyen Tshering who made my trek to Laya such a pleasure. And many thanks to Jigme Tshultim and Karchung Wangchuk for all their help in organising my two trips.

My thanks also to H. E. Dasho Dago Tshering, for his help before I went to Bhutan and for his hospitality at the Paro Tsechu, to H. E. The Chief Justice Dasho Paljor Dorji, to 'Champ', the manager of the Olathang Hotel, and to Paolo and Velda Morisco.

While travelling within Bhutan I received more help and asistance than could ever be acknowledged individually, so thank you very much to *everybody* who let me stay in their houses, or gave me help or hospitality. Special thanks to the Dzongas of Bumthang, Mongar, Tashigang and Gasa, and to Tsinley the assistant Dzongdha in Bumthang; to H. E. Dasho Tshering Dorji the Dzongrab at Gasa, and to Karma Tenpha. Also many thanks to John and Hilary Burslem and to 'Dr Molly', all of the Leprosy Mission, for their help and excellent company.

Outside Bhutan I also received much valuable asistance. My first and most important thank you must be to a very dear friend, Anna Narayan, The Maharani of Cooch Behar, who introduced me to Topga, but who tragically died not very long afterwards. Without her I may never have been invited to Bhutan, and I hope her family will consider this book a small tribute to a very special person, much missed.

In India I would like to thank Anne and Bob Wright, for their endless wonderful hospitality and for their asistance with many projects over the years; Shri Dev Roy and Shri Shamar at Manas; and Toby Sinclair. Thank you also to Shri S. S. Gill at the Indian High Commission in London for his assistance with my permit for Manas, and to Dechen Choden and Marie Brown in New York.

In Britain I was helped with much advice and information, all of which was much appreciated. Many thanks to Michael and Suu Aris, Jenny Devitt, John Blower, Peter Collister, Aidan Crawley, David Gibbs, Dennis Foot, Guy van Strydonck, Mrs Broughton, Malcolm Lyell, Keith Howman, Major Ian Grahame, Jimmy Le Coq and Tom Keith.

Very special thanks must also go to everybody who has helped with the production of the book, most especially to Caroline Taggart at Elm Tree Books who has done such a magnificent job in putting it all together. Thank you, Caroline, very much. Many thanks also to Peter Campbell, the designer, for his patient hard work, and to my agent, Andrew Lownie, who has been marvellous.

Very many thanks also to Olympus UK for their excellent equipment, and for all their support and asistance over several years – it has been a great help. Thank you to Barry Taylor, Mark Thackara, Jason Derrick and Stuart Douglas, and most especially to Ian Dickens.

And a million thanks and a big kiss to my wife, Katie Hickman, especially for being so tolerant of my cameras whenever we are on location. (Her book *Dreams of the Peaceful Dragon*, published by Victor Gollancz, describes our first journey to the far east of Bhutan, and should anybody be interested in signed limited edition prints of any of the photographs in this book they are available through The Special Photographers Gallery, 21 Kensington Park Road, London W14.)

Lastly, a brief note about the text. I have made every effort to check spellings and dates in all the available sources, but as no universally accepted spellings of even some of the most common names exist there is obviously some room for dispute, and I apologise for any confusion caused. When I found conflicting forms I have tended to use the version most commonly found in Bhutanese government publications. Likewise I apologise to those who know Bhutan well for keeping to just one of the many alternative names by which each of Bhutan's great saints are known. Guru Rinpoche is often referred to in Bhutan as Padma Sambhava, for example, but I have not mentioned this in order to keep the text from becoming too cluttered with unfamiliar names. Similarly, when there is an English equivalent for a common Bhutanese term such as 'clown' for 'atsara', I have used the English.

Tom Owen Edmunds
Talycoed, December 1987

Photographic Note

All the equipment I use is Olympus. I have always used Olympus cameras since the OM1 became the first really light SLR and have always found them to be extremely reliable in harsh conditions on location, as well as being excellent optically. I have three bodies, two for Kodachrome 64, my basic stock, and one for Ektachrome 200 or 400, and six or so lenses ranging from 24mm to 400mm. These along with a tripod, a pair of flashes, spare films and a few filters I carry at all times.

The Bhutanese were a delight to photograph whether they had seen cameras before or not. Occasionally they would get terrible giggles, but normally if they saw me they would look for a second and then continue quite unconcernedly with whatever they were doing. Though I can't remember anyone objecting, *every* photograph in this book was taken with permission. This I think is very important, especially in Bhutan which is so unspoilt, as one has a great responsibility as a visitor not to offend local people or culture. Some of the temples I photographed are normally restricted, but in every case I had special permission from the Abbot or Head Lama, otherwise I would certainly not have gone ahead. This is especially true of the statue of the Guru Rinpoche in Kurje Monastery (page 117). When giving permission the Abbot specifically asked that I treat the photographs I took with respect, that I never threw any of them away and that I never placed them on the floor, as it is a most holy statue – and this request I pass on to you in the hope that you will honour it also.

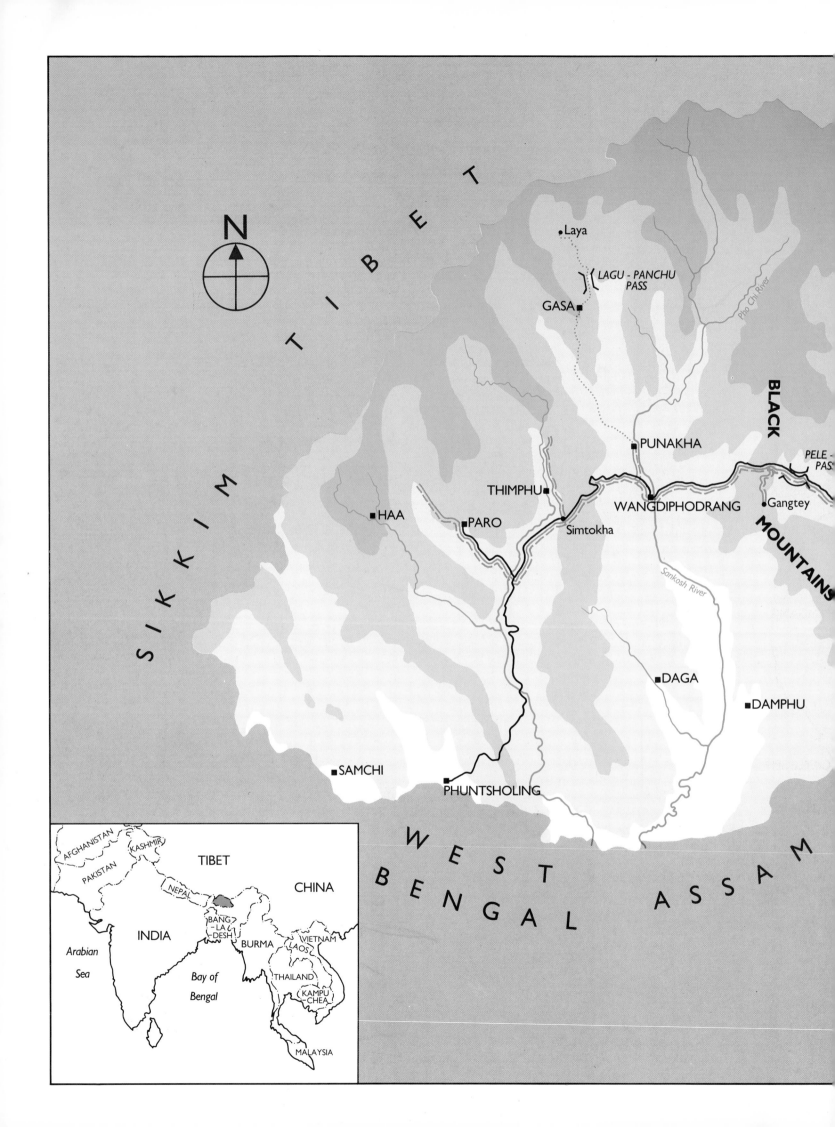

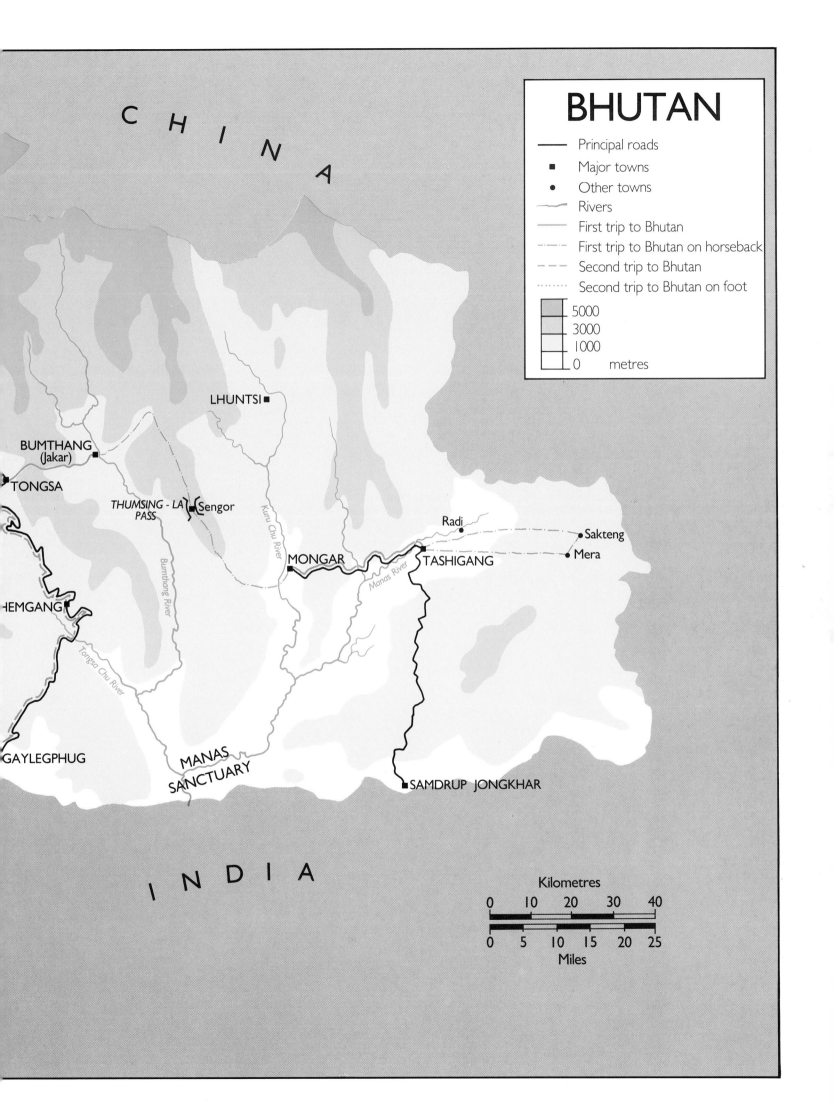

BHUTAN

Legend:
- —— Principal roads
- ■ Major towns
- ● Other towns
- Rivers
- First trip to Bhutan
- First trip to Bhutan on horseback
- Second trip to Bhutan
- Second trip to Bhutan on foot

5000	
3000	
1000	
0	metres

CHINA

LHUNTSI

BUMTHANG (Jakar)

TONGSA

THUMSING - LA PASS Sengor

Radi

Sakteng

Mera

Kuru Chu River

MONGAR

TASHIGANG

Bumthang River

Manas River

HEMGANG

Tongsa Chu River

GAYLEGPHUG

MANAS SANCTUARY

SAMDRUP JONGKHAR

INDIA

Kilometres

0   10   20   30   40

0   5   10   15   20   25

Miles

Tashichho Dzong, the 'Fortress of the Glorious Religion', catches the first light of a new day. Dzongs are the ancient fortress monasteries from which Bhutan is governed. Tashichho Dzong in Thimphu, the capital of the Dragon Kingdom, dates from the twelfth century but was largely re-built by the late king. It now houses both parliament and the central monk body.

A senior monk walks through the courtyard of the monastic section of Tashichho Dzong (right), while nearby two monks peer out of a window elaborately decorated with traditional designs (above). The Dzong is the headquarters of His Holiness the Jey Khempo, Head Abbot of Bhutan, and up to 2000 monks.

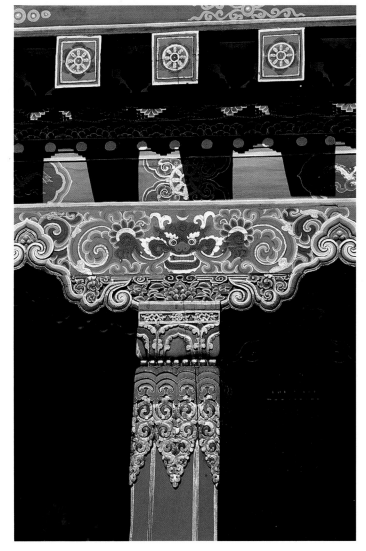

Covered with butter lamps and flanked by elephant tusks, the altar of a temple inside the Dzong is watched over by a huge golden statue of Guru Rinpoche. In Bhutan, the Guru is revered second only to the Buddha himself.

An animal head, carved from wood, snarls from the walls of Tashichho Dzong (left). While partly decorative, its main purpose is to frighten away evil spirits.

No detail of the Dzong is without some divine symbolism; this pillar bears the fearsome visage of the Thunder Dragon itself (right).

Three young novice monks take part in a puja (religious ceremony) in a temple in Tashichho Dzong. Beads of grain,
thrown as an offering to Buddha, are caught in the shafts of sunlight

A nun takes a break from formal ceremony to visit the shops in Thimphu's main street, but her acts of devotion continue.
In one hand she fingers beads while in the other she spins a prayer wheel. As the prayers written on the side revolve,
so they are offered to Buddha and some merit is earned.

Thimphu's main street is lined with shops, brightly painted with mythological animals and abstract designs, beautiful examples of decoration common to every Bhutanese house. To buy something you simply lean in through the window and point to whatever you require.

On Sundays attention moves from the sedate main street to the noisy confusion of the market. Here a Tibetan store-holder shelters from the midday sun. Racially similar to the Bhutanese, the Tibetan refugees who now live in Bhutan are best distinguished by their long hair, which the women plait and tie up over their heads with a coloured ribbon.

A young girl selling vegetables wears a kera, the traditional dress worn by all Bhutanese women. It consists of a single piece of woven cloth wrapped around the body and held at the shoulders by two silver clasps.

The wide range of goods available at the Sunday market even includes a blessing from this lay monk. Not attached to any particular monastery, lay monks can often be found setting up their portable shrines at markets and festivals.

A little girl (above) waits patiently for her mother, while a wandering Holy Man (right) surveys the colourful commotion of the Sunday market.

A detail from a wall painting in Simtokha Dzong, just outside Thimphu. It is part of a 'Wheel of Life' which depicts the different realms of reincarnation. One is the realm of the hungry ghosts, destination of the greedy, and another Hell itself, depicted here with a man having his tongue pulled out and ploughed on.

The Memorial Chorten, built to honour the memory of the late king, looks out over the hills which surround the capital, towards Simtokha Dzong.

A residence of his majesty the king (above) stands beside the Wang Chu River in Thimphu, while close by a typical Bhutanese house in the same style rests amongst the contours of its terraces (right).

The hills in the Thimphu Valley are full of
ancient sacred temples. En route to
Phajoding, a lone temple surrounded by
prayer flags is revealed by a momentary
parting of the monsoon mist (above),
while on the way to Tangu Monastery the
early sun strikes only the tallest blue pines
on a thickly wooded hillside (left).

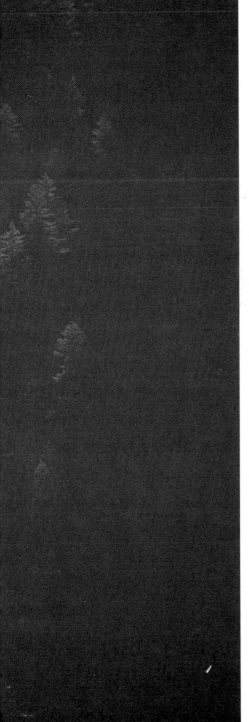

A monk pauses in the courtyard of Tangu Monastery next to a massive prayer wheel. Secluded at the top of the Thimphu Valley, Tangu is one of the oldest and most sacred monasteries in Bhutan (right). Built in the thirteenth century, as one of the two original Drukpa monasteries, it is here that the monks come to perfect the ancient discipline of levitation.

Inside Tangu a monk prepares ritual cakes (tormas) for a puja. Used for all religious ceremonies, tormas are made of flour and butter as an offering to Buddha. The various colours and shapes have important symbolic meaning: here the circular designs represent lotus flowers and the pointed top the sword of wisdom.

A lion guards the entrance to Cheri Monastery (right). Standing close to Tangu, Cheri (above) was founded in 1619 by the first great ruler of Bhutan, the Shabdrung. He was residing here in 1627 when he received two Jesuit priests, the first westerners ever to see Bhutan.

The first day of the Paro Festival, the greatest Tsechu in Bhutan, is held in one of the cobbled courtyards of Rimpung Dzong. It consists of five days of spectacular masked dances and religious allegorical plays unchanged for centuries. Tsechus are very much living festivals: a chance for the community to gather, both to witness the teachings of the Buddha, and to celebrate.

After the first day, the Paro Tsechu moves to a large outdoor courtyard near the Dzong.
Dances are performed by the monks from Rimpung Dzong, the Royal Dance Troupe and local folk
dancers. Above, the Royal Dancers perform the Kyecham.

In the Dance of the Three Kinds of Ging a dancer, holding the stick of wisdom, leaps while pursuing a demon. Introduced by the great Pema Lingpa in the fifteenth century, this dance demonstrates how to subdue demons with magic.

From their vantage point on a balcony overlooking the courtyard, monks of all ages delight in the Tsechu (above), a break from the rigours of their usual daily routine. Jesters provide light relief between the more serious dances, such as the Dance of the Terrifying Deities (left). The gods, in their terrifying form, encircle the enemies of Buddhism, leaving Guru Rinpoche in his form as Dorji Dragpo, the 'Fierce Thunderbolt', to commit their ritual murder.

Many of the huge crowd (right) will have walked for days from their villages in the surrounding hillsides to attend the Paro Tsechu, carrying their own food with them. It is a chance to make friends and show off their finest festival clothes.

The ghostly Dance of the Lords of the Cremation Grounds (above), who protect the eight cremation grounds at the edge of the cosmic mandala, demonstrates how through good deeds you may attain a happy re-incarnation.

Two characters from the epic Dance of the Judgement of the Dead. It is more a morality play than a dance, vividly depicting the Day of Judgement that everybody must eventually face. A monkey-headed helper (above) aids the Lord of Death in his judgement by weighing the good and evil deeds on a scale. A white god speaks up for the man's good deeds, while the devil (right) enthusiastically details his sins.

Clowns are the most popular characters in the Tsechu (above). Not only do they provide slap-stick entertainment between the dances, but also they will often join in the dances and exaggeratedly mimic their every move.

Each day starts with a procession (left) of the senior monks, the musicians and the dancers, from their quarters in the Dzong (seen behind) to the courtyard. The other monks follow along behind in descending order of seniority and height.

The timeless face of a Bhutanese dancer whose job it is to escort and dance beside the procession waits patiently in the Dzong for the procession to assemble (right).

Even the Head Abbot joins the procession, unmistakable in his skull cap and bright orange robes (below).

On reaching the courtyard this young monk, with his ceremonial drum and beautifully embroidered cloak (above), will process around it once before taking his place with the other musicians in the gallery.

One of the most sacred moments of the Tsechu is the arrival of the golden-masked figure of Guru Rinpoche, surrounded by his Eight Manifestations (above). Revered as the Second Buddha, he sits under his canopy while people come down to the courtyard to receive his blessing. A young monk, one of the escort of fairies, probably attending his first Tsechu, pushes back his mask for a better look (right).

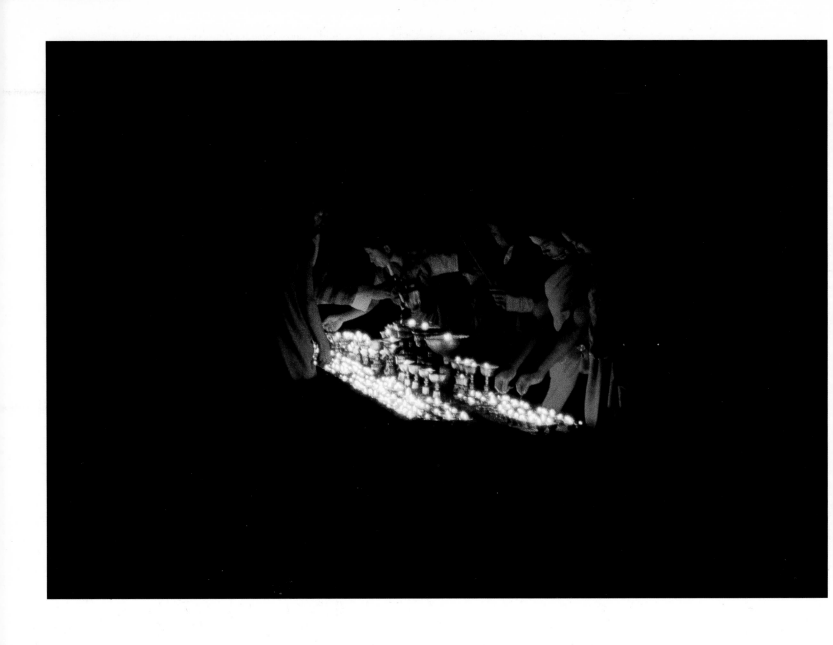

The climax of the festival comes before dawn on the fifth day when, in the presence of the entire monk body, a huge Thanka is lowered, depicting Guru Rinpoche and his Eight Manifestations. Over three hundred years old, this exquisite Thanka is so sacred that it is believed that the mere sight of it can be sufficient to attain nirvana. During the night monks lay out an altar in front of the Thanka (above) and as dawn breaks they perform the Shugdel ceremony, which includes the taking of a ritual meal of blessed food (right).

*To avoid possibility of it fading, the Thanka, displayed just once a year for a few hours, must be put away before the sun
can strike it (above). It is painstakingly lowered, lovingly wrapped in silk and then stored until the next
Tsechu, watched all the way by a young boy in a golden kho (right).*

A covered bridge leads to Rimpung Dzong in Paro, known locally as 'the Heap of Jewels'. On the hill behind, its protective watchtower is illuminated against a thunderous sky, affording just a glimpse of the dragon.

In the spring the shrunken Paro River flows between parched brown hillsides, awaiting the summer rains (right). The ancient 'Temple of the White Horse', dating from the fifteenth century, stands at the base of hills too steep to cultivate.

Further up the Paro Valley the land flattens into a broad fertile plain, sculptured by terraces and dotted with distinctive Bhutanese houses (above).

In summer the Paro Valley is transformed. Rice can be grown at up to eight thousand feet, and the fertility of the land is reflected in the size of the houses (above). This scene with its temples, chortens, prayer flags and paddies is typical of Bhutan.

An old farmer (right), in his rough home-spun kho, rests for a while on the narrow pathway leading to his home.

Religion is part of everyday life for all Bhutanese. In Paro a man walks in a clockwise direction round a temple, spinning prayer wheels as he goes (above), while in Punakha a monk stays on through the heat of summer to look after Punakha Dzong, which is the winter residence of the Jey Khempo.

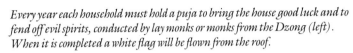

Every year each household must hold a puja to bring the house good luck and to fend off evil spirits, conducted by lay monks or monks from the Dzong (left). When it is completed a white flag will be flown from the roof.

From the balcony, two boys survey the main courtyard of Rimpung Dzong (above). Possibly they are two brothers – the elder visiting the younger novice monk.

Takstang Monastery (right), perched near the top of a sheer three thousand foot cliff, is Bhutan's most holy shrine. It is here that Guru Rinpoche, who brought Buddhism to Bhutan, landed in 747 A.D. astride a flying tiger.

Near to 'The Tiger's Nest', a tiny hermitage clings to a crack in a vertical rock face (above). To achieve greater spiritual insight, the devout will retreat to meditate in such a location for three years, three months, three weeks and three days.

An all too frequent storm throws an eerie light over a terraced hillside near Wangdiphodrang (above), and sends a group of prayer flags on a promontory into a noisy frenzy (right). The flags, with prayers printed on the cloth, are placed on an exposed place so that when they are ripped by the wind the prayers get carried up to heaven.

A lone lily heralds the coming of spring (above) and is echoed by the intense young green of a precipitous wooded hillside above Punakha (right). The route to the north, and ultimately Tibet, starts here in the Pho Chu Valley, and follows a landscape which Samuel Turner described in the eighteenth century as 'Nature in its most gigantic and rudest form.'

The north of Bhutan is covered by some of the tallest and most inhospitable peaks of the Great Himalaya. Few have names and even fewer have been climbed. They remain the Abode of the Gods.

*A sacred mountain towers over Gasa Dzong, which guards the route to Tibet (above). Built in 1649 by the Shabdrung,
it has been the scene of legendary victories over invading Tibetan hordes.*

Beyond Gasa lie valleys and hills which rest for half the year under a crisp cloak of snow (left).

Over the Laga Panchu Pass stands a landscape untouched by man.

One of the few villages to eke a living out of the frozen stony soil of the far north is Laya, clinging to the hillside just a few miles from the border with Tibet (above). Trails are left in the snow by the women dumping baskets of manure in piles on the fields (right).

A rough-hewn wooden figure stands at the gateway to Laya (right).

In the gathering gloom and quickening snow a man returns from the fields with his plough over his shoulder.

The people of Laya are of direct Tibetan descent and have a different language and dress to the rest of the Bhutanese. The women wear patchwork skirts, dark shawls and conical straw hats (right).

*With the mountains of Tibet towering behind a cluster of houses, two Laya men, in their distinctive fur hats,
plough their fields with a pair of huge shaggy yaks (right).*

*The spring is a time of intense activity in Laya. Both men and women work in the fields, leaving the grandparents to
look after the children (above). As in all Bhutanese households, everybody has a role to play in family
life, providing a strong bond of mutual respect.*

*A fierce wet wind whips hair across the face of a young girl carrying manure to the fields in a woven basket on her back
(left). Hardened to the cold, the people of Laya continue to work even through blizzards. Respite comes only with the
dusk, when a cauldron of scalding water to wash in, a log fire and a meal of yak meat
provide a welcome contrast to the rigours of the day (above).*

In the heart of Bhutan the harvesting of barley is still done communally by the oldest traditional method using two sticks. One stick is placed on either side of a few ears, the ends are held and then jerked upwards. Overlooked by a small chorten, cattle follow behind grazing the remnants.

The golden roofs of Gangtey Monastery declare it to be one of the very holiest places in Bhutan. Built on a secluded outcrop in the centre of a huge circular valley, it is the residence of one of the re-incarnations of Buddha.

Located in the Bumthang Valley, the spiritual heartland of Bhutan, the Kurje Temple is another of Bhutan's most sacred monuments. Built by King Sindhu after he was converted to Buddhism by Guru Rinpoche, it houses the largest statue of the Guru in Bhutan (right).

Two Dzongs dominate the centre of Bhutan, Jakar Dzong, 'The Castle of the White Bird', in Bumthang (right) and the vast Tongsa Dzong, historic seat of the kings of Bhutan. All Dzongs conform roughly to the same traditional pattern but are constructed without plans or nails. Inside Tongsa Dzong young monks practise the trumpet before a puja (left).

Away from the Dzongs and the festivals one is quickly immersed in Bhutan's countryside, where the great majority of the population lives. It is a landscape and a way of life unaltered for centuries.

Notched into a tree amongst the fields, a rough phallic symbol evokes the powers of the Divine Madman to protect the crops from evil spirits (left). A home-woven basket full of freshly cut hay boasts his success in neighbouring fields (below).

Prayer walls (right) can be found along even the smallest pathways. The red band signifies that it is a religious object, and holy images or prayers carved on stone are set into the side. Merit is gained by walking round in a clockwise direction.

A girl washes clothes in the outflow of a water-driven prayer wheel. It is an ingenious way to earn merit: a prayer wheel with paddles at the bottom is placed in a chorten built over a stream, and as the water turns the wheels so the prayers are offered.

Merit, more temporal than spiritual, is also gained by this young girl carrying a huge basket of barley back from the harvest.

In the village, after being beaten with a stick, the barley is winnowed to sift the grain from the chaff. The barley is scooped into a flat basket, then scattered, allowing the wind to blow the lighter chaff away.

Elsewhere in the village an old woman attends to the less seasonal task of milking (right), expertly squeezing a jet of warm milk into the wooden bucket below.

From his lookout on the first floor of his house a small boy surveys this flurry of activity.

Performing his daily chore, a young boy collects a handful of sticks to light the hearth.

A beautiful young country girl, in her best kera, rests by the wayside after a long walk to the nearest town to sell grain.

The jungle-clad foothills of Bhutan rise from the pebbled shores of the Manas River. Manas Game Sanctuary, in the deep south of Bhutan, borders with India and has a sub-tropical climate.

6. South: Jungle-clad Foothills

A significant proportion of the population of southern Bhutan is of Nepali origin. A Nepali Bhutanese mahout guides a patrol of forest wardens on elephant back into a clearing in the jungle (right). Elephants are the safest and most practical mode of transport in the jungle.

A typically tropical buttressed tree-trunk in Manas, not found in the colder north of Bhutan (above).

Though it is sometimes possible to see tigers, Manas is most famous as the home of the world's rarest monkey, the magnificent golden langur, whose global range is restricted to a small patch of forest on the Bhutanese side of the river.

Sunset over the Manas River.

The east of Bhutan is a mysterious land, seldom seen by foreigners and little known even in the west of Bhutan. Just over the fearsome Thumsing-La Pass, which separates central from eastern Bhutan, the impenetrable veil of mist parts, just for a second, to reveal a solitary tree.

In the village of Sengor an annual ceremony is held to bless the crops. The sacred texts are taken from the temple, wrapped in fine cloth and encased in planks of wood, then processed through the fields of buckwheat. The procession is led by two boys carrying flags (above) and ends with the only two adults, playing cymbals and a conch shell. Although the texts are extremely heavy, the children who carry them slung over their backs for several hours (right) hardly seem to tire.

Two monks look out of a window in Mongar Dzong, the first Dzong in eastern Bhutan (above).

In the courtyard of the Dzong young novice monks rest between lessons (below). Novices can be taken in as young as five or six years old. They start by learning the holy texts by heart, chanting the verses out loud while rocking back and forwards, sitting in long lines in dim incense-filled temples (right)

A prayer painstakingly carved on to a stone set in the side of a prayer wall in eastern Bhutan.

A sculptured mosaic of newly planted paddyfields reflects a mottled sky.

Near the village of Radi, east of Tashigang, an old lady pauses to adjust her bundle of firewood (top right), while close by a man finishes gathering in his maize (above). But most of the community are occupied planting the paddies (right). Two men help the bullocks on to the next terrace in order to flatten the soil, recently ploughed and flooded, so the women following behind can plant the rice.

*Near Radi, a cluster of houses and prayer flags, set in fields of maize, perches protectively over emerald paddies
etched into the massive contours of a Himalayan foothill (above).*

*At the height of the rainy season a peasant farmer weeds and thins a healthy growth of rice. Rice is the staple food of all
Bhutanese, eaten in enormous quantities with a strong chilli sauce, three times a day.*

A young girl straightens up while thinning a paddy, to shout a greeting to someone on the path below.

Archery, Bhutan's national sport, is the chief form of recreation (right). Celebrations will often be accompanied by an archery match preceded by months of practice. Local contests, renowned for fierce though usually friendly competition, are a highlight of the village year.

In the most easterly tip of Bhutan lives a little-known tribe of nomadic yak-herders called the Bragpas, very different from other Bhutanese. Their barbaric appearance, especially of the men who wear animal skins over their clothes, belies a more gentle nature. Here in Mera, the smaller of the two main villages, a village meeting is called to debate an important issue, attended by both men and women.

A typical Bragpa household in Mera. Buckwheat dries on a mat outside, while under the eaves wood is stacked, a tribute to the Divine Madman hangs down, and the owner weaves cloth on a simple loom watched by a friend.

All but the youngest children spend the day in the close-cropped pastures watching over their herds of yaks (right). The men attend to the yaks on the higher pastures further from the village.

The dress of the Bragpas is unique. Women usually wear a red cape over a home-spun dress pulled in tightly at the waist (opposite), though it is not uncommon to see them wearing the animal skins favoured by most men (above). Even the smallest children wear their own tiny hides (right). Heavy jewellery, especially of silver and turquoise, adorns both sexes, and everybody wears the distinctive yak felt hat. The five points are designed to divert the rains of this stormy region away from the face.

Inhabited only in the summer months, Sakteng is the main Bragpa village. Yaks are grazed on the surrounding pasture and buckwheat grown in enclosures on the flatter land near the rivers. In winter the Bragpas move in tented camps to the lower, more sheltered pastures.

*Very early in the morning a young Bragpa boy walks down from his house high on
the hillside, to Sakteng, carrying with him two silver trumpets
belonging to his family to be used in a puja.*

Two young Bragpa boys take care of their little brother while their mother is out working in the fields (left).

Shortly after dawn there are already several groups of women weeding and thinning the fields of buckwheat on the gentle slopes of the Sakteng Valley (above). This view, looking eastwards from the most easterly point of Bhutan, is the uttermost end of the Land of the Thunder Dragon.

Catching sight of me photographing her thinning a field of buckwheat, an old lady collapses with gales of laughter.
Wherever I travelled in Bhutan I was met with extraordinary hospitality, much good-natured
curiosity and often considerable merriment!